SPATIAL NOSING

New and selected poems

EITHNE STRONG

Poet in Irish and English, fiction writer. A varied life covers taking a university degree after family rearing, participating in publishing, freelance journalism, teaching, work with the media, co-ordinating creative writing courses, giving readings of her work widely and representing Irish writing in Europe—Denmark, France, Germany, Finland, England—the USA and Canada. Awarded travel bursaries. Her work appears in many anthologies. Member of the Executive Committee of the Irish Writers' Union.

Born in west Limerick, she has lived for many years in Dublin where she married, had nine children and was widowed. She has been much involved with the mentally disabled—her youngest son has a mental disability.

She has had eleven books published, and three more are due to appear.

EITHNE STRONG

SPATIAL NOSING
New and selected poems

SALMON  POETRY

First published in 1993 by
Salmon Publishing Limited
A division of Poolbeg Enterprises Ltd,
Knocksedan House,
Swords, Co. Dublin, Ireland.

The moral right of the author has been asserted.

A catalogue record for this book is available from the British Library.

ISBN 1 897648 04 9

Cover illustration by Brian Bourke
Back Cover photograph by Justin Elliot
Cover design by Poolbeg Group Services Ltd
Set by Mac Book Limited in Palatino
Printed by The Guernsey Press Limited,
Vale, Guernsey, Channel Islands.

By the Same Author

Novel: *Degrees of Kindred* (Tansy) "A comedy of manners and ideas, an investigation of the motivations and emotions that lie behind the liberal ethos." Kevin Casey, *Hibernia*.

Narrative Poem: *Flesh: the Greatest Sin* (Runa) "… a seminal poem." Michael Hartnett.

Short stories: *Patterns* (Poolbeg). "Beginning often 'in medias res' she deftly circumscribes the warp and woof of quotidien speech, emotion, will … her empathy assures us again and again that people certainly Rule OK." Aubrey Malone, *Hibernia*.

Cirt Oibre, Fuil agus Fallaí, An Sagart Pinc, Aoife Faoi Ghlas (Coiscéim).

Retrospectively I thank, for their support, Annraoi Ó Liatháin, Rupert Strong, Jonathan Hanaghan, Pádraic Colum, Bertrand Russell, Robert Graves, Hilton Edwards, David Marcus. For ready help with this collection, I thank Mary O'Donnell, Mícheál Ó Siadhail and Jessie Lendennie.

Acknowledgements are due to the following where many of these poems or versions of them have featured: *Poetry Ireland Review, Honest Ulsterman, Broadsheet* (Hayden Murphy), *Irish Pulse, Nial Poems, Nial Magazine, New Irish Writing, The Irish Times, Trinity News, Caritas, Aquarius, Dublin Magazine, Icarus, Westmeath Examiner, Orbis* (UK), *Feathers and Bones* (California), *Hibernia, Stony Thursday Book, Portland Review* (Oregon), *Poems Plain, Shannonside, Linewords, Pebbles, North Dakota Quarterly, Wildish Things, Midland Review* (Oklahoma), *Canadian Journal of Irish Studies, Thinker Review* (Kentucky), *Sleeping with Monsters* (Edinburgh), *Writing in the West, The Salmon, Inti, Comhar, Feasta, WEB, Italian Cultural Institute, Pillars of the House, Four Quartets* (Philadelphia), *Krino, Riverine, Living Landscape Anthology, On the Counterscarp, Gaeliana* (Lille), *Mná na hÉireann, The Flaming Door, Tríonóid 400.*

•

SALMON PUBLISHING LIMITED

receives financial assistance from the

Arts Council/An Chomhairle Ealaíon.

•

O Magnificent Why!

What lives we cobble together for ourselves—my first reaction to Eithne Strong's poetry—lives extraordinary in habit and instinct, in comings and goings through birth, death, and all the in-between rivalries of spirit.

A poet's relationship with words and her relationship with life are inseparable. The technique reflects the vision, the vision reflects the technique, and as we live, we write. As a child, Eithne O'Connell as she was then, knew she would write, and as an adult she did. A series of Quarto publications appeared in the forties, an ambitious undertaking for those years by the young O'Connell and her partner Rupert Strong, both of them working in conjunction with Jonathan Hanaghan, controversial pioneer psycho-analyst. In the fifties she is a contributor to *Tidings*—five hundred copies printed by the Dolmen Press for the Runa Press. In one of the Quartos appears her *Woman of the Ages*:

> "A woman
> serene and beautiful in her gentleness;
> and because of her unworded calm
> and the quiet magnificence of her silence,
> one might not know of her until great suffering
>   came."

Indeed, one might not know of anything until great suffering comes, or great joy. Meanwhile life awaits the poet, and Strong's 1961 collection, acclaimed by Pádraig Colum as the "utterances of the priestess, the druidess, the sybil," is aptly titled *Songs of Living*. Even then, she testifies to human cruelty, and ignorance, the annihilation of a dream that is inevitable *only* when truth is avoided or when indifference sets in. Her *Shepherd the Old* challenges assumptions about sexuality and idealism, and the view that these are the preserve of the young.

Perhaps one should not over-emphasise the druidess or sybil of Pádraig Colum's description: to do so would be to blinker our view of an eclectic mind which has come to grips with living—through marriage, through bearing nine children, through intellectual dialogue, through travelling, through simply seeing what goes on—always assessing with a shrewd and honest eye.

Certainly, like the druidess, Strong's work demonstrates a sensibility which is tolerant of outward conventions, drawing a sheath over these in the way one does—protective pragmatism? Who can say. But there exists a woman who has not over-compromised, who toadies to neither convention, nor fashion, nor ambition, nor posturing. She has had too much to do to be bothered wasting energy on the veneer that is supposed to maintain civilisation. The fires of outrage burn brightly through each collection, fires which temper character and vision with the experience of vulnerability, tenderness, the falterings of children and men and socially approved "nice women"—none of whom escape her scrutiny.

But in today's climate, to call a writer a druidess (no matter how well intended) seems too plausible a label, a dated term which circumscribes rather than illuminates, an escape-hatch description suitable for a woman writer, encoded with the approved subjects with which women who write are supposed to deal.

The poems selected from Eithne Strong's early work, and those from her later collections, *Sarah, in Passing* (Dolmen 1972), *My Darling Neighbour* (Beaver Row Press, 1985) and more recently *Let Live* (Salmon, 1990) are evidence of growing creative powers as experience has deepened. Strong was always wise, but the poems fan out in a multiplicity of directions. Love is a constant theme, right from the early days, but how it has been transmuted by cussed living, bargaining and the brinkmanship of human relationships! The newest material, which includes thrilling poems like *Woad and Olive*, *Tournesol*, *Saturday Morning*, *Nothing Heavenly* and *Spatial Nosings* is tinged with private philosophy, no longer as easily divulged perhaps, but part of a vision which affirms multiplicity and is more tolerant than ever of such.

Diversity of thought and impulse makes these poems radiate humanity, belief and a revelatory sense of justice. The inequities of human relationships is something this poet is particularly adept at exploring, and none too gently either, with flesh locked between the teeth as she tears back to the bone. The culture which she observes and partakes of is a man-made one, largely supported by women who either endure the ways of the despot or else forge their own peace by simply getting on with it. That forging is not one of resignation, so much as an energetic re-appraisal of how best a person can live within the constraints of the world as it is apprehended.

Thus, in *Sarah, in Passing*, although Strong's poems by chance coincided in expression and content with Ireland's feminist stirrings during the 1970s, these are primarily *humanist* pieces which demonstrate how the nuances of an unpolemic feminist perspective are most capable of registering in the poetic, *without becoming propagandist*, and where the vision of a fairer way of being and becoming is presented through one's experience of womanhood or manhood.

Some of this poetry reflects the platitudes of language which mark daily congress. "... a nice woman ... another way/to say a poor uneducated sop."

Children are made to listen to their mother's needs, they too must hear how she cries for stars "as in my callow years." And although ambition is tested and tortured and tempered through a handicapped child, Strong possesses too much artistic integrity not to see the transparency of some of the social and technological products of ambition. In fact, some of the work is textured with a tongue-in-cheek assessment of literary pantheons and merry-go-rounds, of popular bandwagons and "movements," the way status and power are achieved through a prostitution by which one must hold Poetically Correct attitudes in order to be taken seriously! And science too prostitutes—her poem *July '69* opts out of the drooling adulation which surrounded the moon-landings:

"All hail the great scientific Prick!"

She herself acknowledges that human *composition/person to person* is her sphere and not the macro-reflections of the allegedly broader and more global. Yet she is political, and like the better political poets feels no need to announce this, choosing instead to examine prehistory and the twentieth century, seeing no difference at all in the slitting, mutilation and destruction which mars our experience (*Up and Out*).

My Darling Neighbour, over a decade later, shows

a consolidation of interest in matters of identity, both public and private. She questions the learned tendency to avoid self-love and self-praise, indeed breaks a time-honoured rule of classical Western thinking by recognising the wisdom of Narcissus! The identity of writers and artists, which hinges at a superficial level on public acknowledgement, though most vitally on the private mind, is addressed in *Diameter*:

> "there are those certainly
> who ...
> desperately fearful of traceable personal
> > alignment,
> wrap up the clues (obscurity the real essential)."

A consciousness of the physical pervades the work, together with a sensuous delight in a natural world (*Letter to Ireland*) which is always underpinned by cultural connections of one kind or another (including those of intellectual snobbery and ignorance). But most fundamentally of all, finality and dissolution are presences behind all the birthing, loving, moving, working and striving. She celebrates age, and instead of Yeats's *The Dreaming of the Bones*, Strong brings us a slightly irreverent, modernist inversion of literary staples with *The Creaking of the Bones*.

In her 1990 Salmon Publication collection *Let Live*, death is a force in many of the poems—vigorous and healing, provocative but also spawning profound aloneness. The poems *Gaspé to Ottawa* and *However Long That Dark* are poems of courage. No heroics, thanks all the same, but a facing down of death, hand-to-hand combat if you like; yet even that is traced through with the powerfully touching lineaments of love as she urges the "*beloved human*" to search out his courage.

This woman has been everywhere, both in herself and in the world. The external geographies provide constant food for thought in a creatively instinctive mind effervescent with the intellectual need to know and to question. From Thomas Mann country to Tiananmen Square, to the Barrow Estuary or Bloody Foreland, she identifies the thing-in-itself, sometimes tearing through layers of social and historical concealment, other times gently folding back as one would a sectioned peach in order to get to the stone. And if it is bitter, if it is cyanide? So much the better, because Eithne Strong can then understand, and her readers can understand something of the nature of this place we inhabit.

If she seems happier away from Ireland, that's probably because she is. Foreignness, cultural codes not of this island—though different—are nonetheless easier to assimilate. Yet this is where she has lived, loved and achieved. The inversions of form, the unexpectedly broken phrases at line endings which every so often contrast with an accomplished use of end-rhyme (which almost tricks the reader into imagining some kind of conformity and tradition) are further signs of a reactive nature living in the terrain of a physically-cloven society. There are no sonnets, no traditional love-verses, the Aisling does not drift through these poems as the spirit of Ireland unfolds.

At the time of writing this preface, Eithne Strong has just set off on a reading tour of North America. She carries on, bringing vigour and commitment to a written word which is too often one-sided and one-sexed in its allegiance, and narrow in its subject matter. As she says herself:

> "Now, there are so many dead.
> I am tired of competitions,
> spend much time with hindsight.
> Anyone may visit me."

The volume you are about to browse through, dip into, or read with assiduous care, is a special one: it asserts human survival, validates hope, science, literature, and love, through an insistent and confident questioning which rings with private philosophy but never jeopardises the poetic. Life, despite the presence of death, cannot be extinguished:

> "It will be, despite annihilations: in fine,
> because of them? O magnificent why!"

Mary O'Donnell

Part I
from *Songs of Living*, 1961

To My Father 3
Mother and Daughter 4
Synthesis—Achill, 1958 6

Part II
from *Sarah, In Passing*, 1974

Vale et Salve 13
Beauty is in the Eye 14
Confrontation 15
The Mahonys Observed 16
Mrs Mahony's Anniversary Thoughts on
Her Man 18
Bridge of Asses 20
Judess 21
Statement to Offspring 22
Measuring 23
Retarded Child 24
Norms for a Literary Piece 26
Dear Doctor 28
Response to Munch's *Scream* 29
Regeneration 30
Labour Rights 31
Pound in the Pub 33
July '69 34
Credo 36
Academician 38
Regarding Words 39
Spring: Concerning Shape 41
Visionary 42

Part III
from *My Darling Neighbour*, 1985

Necessity for Reverence   47
Diameter   48
Identity   50
Unions   51
Dance to Your Daddy   53
Love Me Tender   55
Library, Section Lit. Crit.   56
The Creaking of the Bones   57
Energy of Jura   59
Blood and Walls   60
Aptitude   63
Between You, Me and the Lamp-Post   64
Letter to Ireland   65
Proposal for Magritte   67
Bottoms   68
Brian Boru and Aurora   70

Part IV
from *Let Live*, 1990

Let Live   75
The Learning Process   77
Peanut Queenie   78
Unapprehended   79
Forces—North Kerry   80
To My Mother   81
Gaspé to Ottawa   83
However Long That Dark   85
Progenitors   86
The Giant's Causeway   87

Bloody Foreland   88
Achill   89
Beara Peninsula   90
Barrow Estuary   91
Dublin Bay   92
Henrietta, Caleb and Issue   93
September Song   95
Hola Verdad!   97
'Counterrevolution'   99
Yellow Joke   101
Thomas Mann Country   102
Bald   104
Liberté, Dublin '89   106
Summer Seine   107
Making   108
Pram   109

Part V
New Poems

Woad and Olive   113
Feet   116
Thinking of Kevin McAleer, Derrida and
Hogan Shea   117
Further Matter for Magritte   119
My Darling Women   120
Fifty Years On   123
Sour   125
Tournesol   126
Masochist   128
Blarney Machree   129
Curves 1 and 2   131
February '92   134

Flying Visit, Finland '92   135
Surviving, Helsinki, Turku '92   137
Brim   139
Circling   140
Points of View   142
Saturday Morning   144
New Departure   146
Constant Kind   147
Nothing Heavenly   149
Spatial Nosing   151

Part I

from Songs of Living, 1961

To My Father

I
had left this land
and turned away
ah! cold of stone:

had sunk well-spring of love
down-sunk
from reach of mind
and wealth of soul
deep in the brown bog from which I sprang
and left it cold.

Primeval ashes of my dead quest
strewn bleak upon the hills
along the twisting glens.
Ah! numb of cold.

But you
would not go away.

You
could not leave these ancient glens and hills
to live the crowded travesty of life
that is our city.

So
you laid your head in final peace
upon the soil from which we came.
Your noble head and fine
and went to sleep
all dignified
and majestic utterly.

Mother and Daughter

You that were
my babe
first mother-joy of mine
so proud I.

Now
You are growing
Beautiful gazelle.

Suddenly
I am the old witch.
The old witch watches
the beautiful gazelle
with hideous eyes of hate.

Matriarch I
in my jealous jungle
stalk tigers
aprowl
for the shapely gazelle.

The bulls flourish their maleness
in the morning air
and snuff for the young odour.
The witch and the tiger
crouch for the smell of blood.

Old witch am I
and tiger too
and godless blood-rite pound in me.

With sad self-knowing
aye, thus can a mother be.

Old swamp of ages
from which we arose
the babe and I.
The devolutionary swirl
sucks ever at my feet:

But yet I hear the singing stars
and the out-bound wind
for the gazelle and me.

Synthesis—Achill, 1958

Do not speak now
because of the beauty
and yet the day must not pass
before I bear witness

No day had been like this day.

You could take my hand
strongly in yours
and with swift purpose
seek to speed me past
my failings; your voice
could tell me how to hold
when weakness drags my traitor self.

But I must go alone
and put my head low upon the heather
and find my strength.

Old druid hills
gird black the sunset sky.
Old old strength of immemorial earth
lies quiet beneath my tangled heart.

Nigh midnight now
yet twilight holds the mystic time.
Heathered wind is light
about the ancient rocks.

Pray.
Yes, I have such need to pray.

Strip now the veils.
Still the mind, the twisting thought.
Hear the inner inner pulse
go slow
slower,
quiet,
still.
Wait for the inward silence.
Now
the naked heart.

The hills abide in ancient strength
against the endless sea.
Old druid hills bide dark
against the western light.

And I
must bear witness
to this midnight tryst.
All through
the sun-drenched drowse of day
I knew a muted urgency of blood
and mind and life
to hold this tryst.

Therefore
it was no sudden thing
that drew me from my bed
into this night that still is day
with lustrous moon gold-red
hung eastward low
and western peaks druid-black
against the sunset sky.

It is midnight now.
New wind down ancient heights
and the voiceless sea.

This tryst with what made me.

Part II

from *Sarah, in Passing*, 1974

Vale et Salve

Down at the edge greyly bleaks tomorrow;
directionless, a sigh spreads every dawn.
Lying in wedding bed already sick with child,
nor room nor bed theirs, nothing of their own
but will to cling and cleave through famine
into an unpromised land.

Outside and away over chill river grass
she had said goodbye old God, had missed
mass the first time ever, had made deliberate
sacrifice to new demanding god, had heard
her mother sob for the soul gone wrong
—with status, and sorrows of ambition,

the mother would have to believe it so;
her father nearly died of puzzled heart:
for the new this marriage was killing old.

Well then newgod, I cleave and cling
through bafflement, lurching, ill and seek
to suck some health from bare of poverty.

Beauty is in the Eye

I do not like your flatpate face
and greedy pushing mouth that laps
up what it may out of my doings
your empty faceflat life that

stares into mine feral curious. You would devour
all that my life has been. Ingest
reptilian findings in your cellar solitariness
where damp deliberate you remain barriered

from warm fellows. Whatever you see with
cold snake's eyes I reject your dart and poke
of spatulate head your clammy coil
about my privacies.

Confrontation

A strange distance in morning faces blankly
close in blood. I look in to say
goodbye. I am off to my important day.
You sit daughters, on either side the table,
your sons on laps, feeding them their little
necessary messes. You talk only
to your sons. So short a time since I
so held you to coo and gladly kiss
messed faces; accept, indulge caprice—
me, the fine maternally.
You, adored, the centre of your tyranny.
Now you stare back at me from adult eyes
that I no more know. Layer upon
layer, you are more unknown to me than
Amazon territory. I make a few inanities,
my silly admonitory jollities to you
through your sons: I am no longer
tolerant of your messiness. You over
indulge them and me you spare
your round brown stare.

As I leave the house the rain
is powder fine—last night it was hail—
first softness of the year in opening trees
where birds liberate.

It seemed like pain in the round lonely eyes
but then, I do not know them anymore.

The Mahonys Observed

Does Mahony get an unfair deal like most only worse?
A man in chase of Truth, he never takes his full of rest
and Truth wears many masks exhausting him to
                                              find her face.

He never stops. His house is swarmed with torments
from his raw and truthwould heart. Only in heaven
will it be known, he said, finding his special Christmas

slippers in the garden pond, his new tie in the jam.
His wife, a sort of literate shrew, no helpmeet, complains:
All of my body's veins are near the surface; they clump

and knot in tumescence, excess of blood against
                                              contraction.
A shrew shrilly at his life's intention: Must I forever
play pretender, never state, for appearances' protection

that you have packed me with seed I never had the urge
to need? And must I halleluia for you who tyrannised
amicably my every year with salutary all-lovingness

which, oddly, never loved helping me on another way?
My plural womb engorged perennially against the sink;
my total energy to breeding went, to battered days'

endeavour, nursing, patienting the chaos of the young.
If this were the full of Mahony's case … but is it
quite? Yes, she hacks at his adamantine moral legs

yet finally closes her most peculiar brand of balm
around his sapphire wounds, and so they jointly meet
the possible days, stubbornly greet untellable
                                        continuum.

Mrs Mahony's Anniversary
Thoughts on Her Man

A testament to you who have
gone one hard way, believing
more of men and life than ever
came into any part of your day
and still believer. A tribute

to your faith (in spite of
my sometimes finding it smack
precious of the goody boy on
Sunday—*that* is gauge of me
in the final estimate): it took

you where violence can never
get, to basaltic constancy
regarding what encountering
in me, ours, others and—hardest—
in your own persistent core,

of barrenness, negation, treachery.
I feel a something now for you
long left euphoria: a kind of
close tough feel, hardcome from
things the years can't name that

carry their own secret witness
to mixed processing in furies,
fevers, the drearier-than-dead
of dim-to-grey; contraries like
acid toned with honey; volte face

of voids and ecstasies. It is
a shrink-dried durable stuff this
unenchanted cool: catalyst to
quotidian doubt and treason. I,
noneuphoric, believe its name is love.

Bridge of Asses

I dread to be that most targetable thing
the ridiculous woman.
So much of me is fair game
for your clever tongue.

You could take any one part of me
and dart. I'll certainly bleed.
Your friends will laugh and you
and they can stand another round.

Fearing all of this I shrink
before your philistine eye.
I'll build protection in my looking
so that seeing me you will not see.

I have my special voice for you
the one that tells you nothing.
You know enough for wit
my very guard is your meat.

Then I face my dread and try
a private promising of bravery:
perhaps today I'll stay the natural woman,
if you like, ridiculous.

Judess

Take off the hair
the flesh and bone,
see the palpitating
brain: you nothing
see, however great
your microscopic lore.

Yet I looked inside
the skin, I searched
my dark just now, saw
there Judas stript
to rope; no sacred
thing beside him

lived: the search,
significance, decayed;
betrayed were all—
mate, mother child;
but treacheried most
horribly, belief in life.

Statement to Offspring

Look, I'll never leave you, issue
of my bone: inside
the marrow's marrow tissue
I am true no matter what.

But I must not be your slave
and do not suck my later life.
I, of sweat and pain have
given, and breaking labour.

Let me be. There is much
I am starving for.
No muffler I to scarf your
years. I cannot aye be shield.

Rebellion? Yes. I am but part
grown. We grow till death.
Let me space. I cry for stars
as in my callow years.

But test me and I'm there.
In the meantime, let me burgeon
whatever else may fruit.
I have suckled without stint.

Let my statement grate whom will.
I am no easy choice.
I never asked to have you
but having, am entirely true.

Just allow me room.

Measuring

I am the sow would like my wallow,
my snore in the sun.
Or I would bar the house and read all day:
be in to none—
Do not disturb.

Sometimes I am very strange to all
my young; they, the foe
inimical to my private schemes, negate ambition.
Yet I must show
endless resource

to their fulfilling, who am the centre
to which cling
their flucuant hate, initial focus of their weight
before they swing
ambivalent load

outside to friendships, teachers, lovers.
Still them, with grunts
and snorts and wallows, I have loved mixed
                                    muddily.
There was never made
the measuring tape.

Retarded Child

I wished him dead
  he came between
        he stopped my moves.

Note his look
  brain in face
        it skews his eyes

it drools his mouth.
  Fool doctor's fault:
        a lack of care

a lack of air.
  Nothing genetic.
        The doctor since dead.

No fault in genes:
  o comfort to pride
        I hope myself right.

Posterity
  might hate my guts
        for showing their mates

the bred regress
  the faulty dread.
        So I resort

in my foolish time
  to clearing guilt
        a useless game.

It has been said
  his, a handsome head
      when eyes and mouth are happy.

I have wished him dead
  in my coward part.
      My fiery plans

he has cut athwart.
  My blazing drive
      he braked dead stop.

I burned with schemes
  cruel mighty dreams.
      Reality

has been quite other:
  he has tested me
      to my miser heart

whose greedy aim
  was glory, fame.
      My own prisoner, I,

before ever he.
  My one release;
      to pledge his need.

On escape so bent
  the chains I've rent
      serving committedly.

Norms for a Literary Piece

I took a beansprout
out of Swift, it barely
missed the sewer—I was
reading Austin Clarke's
memorial piece—and fell
instead on Cain; my crazy
child (who may be wise
beyond brains) had gone
to sane Cross Avenue
where truly decent people
in steadfast sanity
coach him for Cubs. I am
humble before their zeal.
I was (reading Clarketyping)
eating a Take-away Special
from The Great Wall, Main
Street, Blackrock; hardfried
egg on top of mixed-up
dubiosity of rice (all day
he—impact of Wisdom?—
crashed my back, jerked
away from tapping keys
my hands, trying to spell
out Clarke on Swift), slices
of pork, excess of monosodium
glutamate—an official from
Swift's Hospital with concern
for dietetics warned me once
against that glutamate but I
like the sound of the name,
the taste of the sound—

not to forget beansprouts:
the last one dropped upon
the Gulliverian urinal, plonk
into the Queen's private
apartment. O enigmatic aim,
deadline literary special,
jigsaw mind, crazy frame—
Shake on it, Swift, old bean.

Dear Doctor

It was a harmless thing he did
boasting newcome knowledge.
'Manic depressive' glibly said;
she showed apparent courage.

'Of course, the term' he generalised
'this one or that evinces ...
symptoms that an extra strain
leads to electrodes, pincers.'

'In dull suburbia,' he glibbed,
'are wives tied up in tension.
In offices are droves of men
who barely can malfunction.'

'But we could put them right again:
tablets, shocks and needles ...
the stigma hardly matters now.'
Confidentially he wheedles.

That night she burst into his place.
Her maddened eye hung down her cheek.
She threw her heart right at his face,
His sheets were spattered bones and brains.

Response to Munch's *Scream*

See
my middle-class bastions
—scarcity I detest;
the order and method of my house
—I abominate a scatterbrain;
decorum and reserve my manner
—one abhors gush.

But
ten times a day
I assail the walls of sanity
tear comfort raw
slash at padded ease
wreck the engulfing cloy.
Secretly I am lunatic.

Hear
I must shatter the void
rend to maniac necessity
beyond the stale of habit
burst to crazy power:
comfort chokes in muffling tyranny
the scream is my survival.

Regeneration

Let me out. I'm rising out of death's skull.
Aha, old devil's dower I have victoried.
I leave you to the morning: it deals
with every death and Spring defeats the catafalque.

You see I must believe in resurrection.
This is it. Now. I was dead and am alive.
Hello eternity. I can die no more horrific
death than I have died. No hell beyond

the horrors of myself that murdered
every life; saw death in every pregnancy
of dog and nut and man. Found death
the ever death. Come bomb, come

my most killing hate, life lives outside
the blasting skull. Computer is not final.
I cannot give you proof of course,
I merely have arisen.

Labour Rights

Recently I was given a remarkable cover for my bed.
With cool deliberation—lying on its purple and red—
I consider felicities of balance. Having latterly made

claims for proportion, I am arranging now a late
levelling towards idleness of one sort, offset
against consuming body-busyness that ate

the previous years. I am contriving barefaced
confrontation with dictums bred, intersticed
with my out-of-sight self, old tyrannies

like Idleness tempts the devil. There are now therefore
days when I am a director of operation, lounging hour
at a stretch, book in hand, giving the nicely-phrased
                                                      order,

supine on my purple and scarlet. My cleaner clearly
believes me bone lazy
but as to that I am easy—

such conveyed indictment would have been a bother
at one time; its oblique compulsion would
                              have made me founder
in ostentatious activity, seek exoneration from the other.

But now let her scrub—she has all respect of my
                                          experience;

she also has a mop with a lever although I did the
                                                    job knees
and hands way. I am easy that she battle muck and,
                                                    grease:

I have total work myself implementing my campaign
for physical nondoing, tenaciously expanding mental
                                                    gain,
that skimped necessity, my long overdue, my
                                        bone-idle claim.

Pound in the Pub

The son of a famous image
recites the poetry of Pound;
his father's son indeed,
in love with self-projection:
reflexes in fine variance
of voice, as much display
of him as Pound.

This beautiful phraser,
indubitably agile,
wears a cardinal bland hat,
his indispensable crown
on the plastic pub throne
above the beer:
he rouses me stone cold.

July '69

Now this is a celebration all night long
for the American moon off the Boul. Mich.
At three and four and five this hooha hoo:
A falstaff negro swings his two-foot fish
around his girl and dances in the loo,
lets the door clap with a fruity hot laugh,
jolly Frenchmopolitan of the sixth floor.
Overhead gay ablutions: the spick Algerian who
expanded conversation in the corridor
and invited me to his Tangier home
then called my child mignonne.
The man we met on the train from Rome
sings of his artist's house in Greece;
I liked his chat for accent's sake—
is it not molto molto this technology age?—
but that insinuation outside his door …
The Chinese cafe plied madly all night
making shouting money no matter what:
saki dishwash noodles and duck
spread miasma oriental and gallic.
Television everywhere, blasting the courtyard air.
O dance and laugh and sing and shout
for the moon is caught.
The Americans have made her.
All hail the great scientific prick!
I sink my fangs in my child's corpse
I roast my frailbone brother's bowels
I gorge on famine villages.
A feast by any other name of course—
Russian salad is splendid with Maryland

chicken and peaches and lychees
from Mao.
Let us drink to the blended consortium.
The moon is our millennium.

Credo

I feel witness
to unchangingness
as well as change.

If I incline to
leave unmirrored
political moil, it is because

the human composition,
person to private person,
is my sphere, my particular

theme. In brief—
the things of state—
bland blue-suit smile,

smooth-shirt doubledo
(we beg true blue but
have them shot by dark);

lobbying;
feather-nesting; high inflate
of rigmarole; vigilant spite

that splits the nose
to spoil the party face—
all these things I have to see

as but reflections
in macro of doings round
the micro centre. As people

pattern in private
so, unchangingly, will they
projected in their public scale.

The central attitude
is inexorable: there is no
escape; life demands encounter

with figures like
fathers, brothers, lovers
rivals, mistresses, mothers, wives.

Inevitably national
and international are but larger
shapes of interpersonal procedures:

appetites and checks
that flux around the swallowing
demand of predatory devouring 'Me'.

Large happenings
in the state wear secondary
coverings. My bent is primary.

Academician

A time or two when, inevitably, we
discussed your talks, I said you
were like a guinea-pig. Something
in your stance called up the image
of that animal. Come to think now,

it was odd how: you were the don,
instance of conceptual decorum,
marking dry point in removed irony.
No pig in that. Your solid little
block of head, without much neck,

squatted erudition near to shoulders
that spoke the man of books. No pig
in books. Yet that was it, your
sudden upward head into the hunch
of book-crouched flesh, there was

the guinea-pig, as indeed was he
there bright, surprising me, in your
small academically sly eye. I was
quite prepared to parody: you were
victim, my offering to general laughs,

compensatory to my unstated need,
my consciousness of lack gauged
by your defeating store. But
then I found you, later tested,
truly kind, and was defeated more.

Regarding Words

In this amorphous flux I, at this point
sharply needing the particular form
of noform, celebrate
the unfinished edges advancing beyond
the frame that no dogmatic limn
ever satisfactorily defined;
resume a blurred commencement.

Death has been around so much this week:
a number of people peculiarly set in
the unpattern of my flock
have died, which makes it difficult
to lapse with quite usual unplan
into the lame of eat
and sleep and masturbatory talk

that is my normal limp into nofreedom.
Having thought considerably about cold
clay, irrevocable clod on suppurating palm,
I link the daily palliative with such;
envisage flesh once known by hand
and look, breaking, after black touch
of deep days down, into the grim

of stenching sores: once-known flesh,
repository of most I ever felt
regarding unsaid push
of words concerning hands, shafting life,
renewal of young. My mother soon must
die, and I have brinked the cliff
before which life seemed endless

and decay impossible, I salute the imperishable
bone; requiring the form of no ruled dimension,
I reject, though not unlovingly,
the attempted words of all presuming to interpret,
then using words myself, can only run
their limit, yet indefinably unite
with whom presumes and the future unshape.

Spring: Concerning Shape

Suddenly, in an indifferent week, they troop the grass
triangle, fulfilling inexorable thrust to their fifteen
day fragility. Their willynilly gleam leans south
before an absolute north wind that crocus-spears, that
snowdrop-bells their white, their gold obeisance

to the cold hard sun. One precise green oval away
the little dogs yap in a frantic room. Somewhere
is a locked place in the research department; sun
has come to claim a new day's revenue and dogs smell
death in the sharp clear light. Students traipse

the southward path. Stronger than flowers they hold
their backs against the wind but obey the group-troop
to knowledge: fragments stripped from tissue of dog.
(When obscene knives obliterate what was the shape
of dog, where finally goes the speared corruption

that was a yap, a laugh, a yelp in fear, the entrail-
dung in plastic perpetuation of bags, boxes, bins?)
Dissection is like breathing, they must do it for
survival. A race is on; the oxygen cake gets eaten.
When they have passed, six kicked crocuses turn satin

necks flatly to the west. Beyond the terror of dogs
cranes swing identifiable loads to heaven, building
the foreseeable time. Engines squatly cough a lethal
fume for general diet. The circular span proceeds
holding links of blood and root and force, indefinitely.

Visionary

He stands on a mental pinnacle
and sees the far achievable milk
and honey. He would sufferingly die
and gladly, believing
in his pilgrimage
to such earthly ultimacy where survival
is of another order and manifold loves
have found accepted levels, chiefly,
where women have learned the love of women
in heterosexual totality;
where flesh is not territory
for a new competitive high
in orgasm but for cherishing even
humped limped toothless brainless.
He seeks an offering hand, a bonded few
who, though inevitably maimed,
could yet prove the triumph
of consolidating love, the harvest.

Marriage, he said, as prototype is
on the way out. The legal form persists,
ensures some lame security, an uncertain prop
to our manipulative modes. But appetites
outleap laws and we who break the elements,
fly to Mars, control nothing yet, who from
the start have not understood our own control.
The pill means fuck, genitalia for sensation
merely, a turn-on, defeating try at titillation.

I envisaged something different far as leap
out of possessive marriage. I imagined

an abidingness, a permanence through
multifarious experiment; a sustaining of lives
engendered, where homosexual and lesbian had
toleration and clear significance—best
understood, love of one's own sex could mean
society's cement not fragmenting, could be
subsumed in a wider love transcending

jealousy: *I might like you until*
             you threaten to diminish me.
             My name is still Amoeba: in
             my jelly space you are
             competitor for my portion.

and age: *He is past his climacteric*
             she, her menopause—
             bring on the euthanasia.

and maim: *How did he manage it with his one leg?*
             Does your probing tongue turn sour
             discovering false teeth?

all that, accepted and transcended
in place of legal mechanistics.
Love is not commercial goo nor hippy easy.
I see it as meaning the strong stuff
of lastingness in flexible but quite
unsloppy modes that provide parentage
for children no matter whose their genes.
It could dissolve the segregating walls
that box in people, that emphasise
the desiccated sufficiencies,
lonely duplication of consumer goods.

43

Part III

from My Darling Neighbour, 1985

Necessity for Reverence

O potato that I peel
I am made to know
your raw appeal
insidious, oddly,
not blunt nor coarse
as might one
expect from something so
crudely sprung;
in some peculiar fashion
you quietly present
your claim for reverence,
you, cockeyed, swarth,
supporter of my family;
I feel a vague design
holds me in curious link
with you whose peel
I strip while the Taoiseach
sits in council.

Diameter

Confessional is out of fashion.
Objectivity is in. In spite of mode,
however, it must be said never has one

the truly objective met
in issues from the poets' circuit.
there are those certainly

who give to understand they are
presenting the cool rationale
and, desperately fearful

of traceable personal alignment, wrap up
the clues (obscurity the real essential),
imagining meanwhile

themselves into a future filed,
cross-referenced, in countless
Pee aitch Dee theses:

Joyce and Yeats—so why not me?
Supporters, they, of the industry
in abstraction, par excellence,

concretised in Molly Bloom's
vagina—was it concave or convex?
Decades hence, imagined students

will anxiously peruse
the possible derivations
of such and such allusions:

a First or Double First
could teeter on the clinch
of fresh interpretation

duly screwed
by striving substantion
in close adherence to the text.

Did she masturbate the liver?
Did he fuck his daughter—
excuse me—give expression

to incestuous inclinations?
Therefore, preciously, some
fabricate convoluted structures,

cross-layering sign
and opaque symbol since
out of nothing nothing comes;

and thus gets proferred alleged cool
anonymity of the thing-in-itself
so ultimately confessional.

Identity

One-eyed Spring gone wrong and a rather
crazy—by district style—neighbour
having a go at her lawn, long-abandoned:
things just here are not in approved plan;
her odd-bod shave leaves behind
long swathes lumpily lying where,
quick, the small girls—newbreed mites,
latter-day, unfathered kind—rush to play;
quick into it they run, not letting
lie but running lumps of lying grass
abandonedly into the sky; high,
jumbling sky; wildish things these—
little newbreed Irish girls, scarce
parented, not to be grooved into
rectangular requisite. And I,
long tooth of expected sanity, see
from my high seat, my supposed sober
chair, second-storey; see, and feel,
in sudden flash, newfleshed;
rejoice, identified with bastards,
grass, odd-bod, confused sky; I, seeing me
not at all made to regular shape,
who privately am
according to suburban norm
quite ab.

Unions

Mrs Janet Doorly
stood by
the machine
bestowing washing.
The big sheets—
six-year guarantee,
polyester, and cotton—
had to be
bundled in a special way,
corners to centre,
to prevent
the sodden ball
that would knock hell
inside the machine.
As Mrs D rolled up
the ageing stuff—
five years she had them—
flakes and fluff
flew in the swirling beam
of morning chilly sun
coming backdoor in.
She considered removedly
the flying motes
seeing therein atoms
of Mr D, herself,
their shedding young:
bits of dead Doorly stuff
inconsequentially floating
through morning
keeping company
with particles

of scaled commercial sheet,
sometimes settling
on the kitchen floor
of striving blue hygiene.
Mrs D walked
in the united atoms
reflecting fractionally
on the myriad
necessary deadnesses
that proceed
throughout the living day.
Mixed with
her short domestic spurt
was a customary cloud
of philosophic indulgence,
conceptual fog,
requiring no clarity.
Assuredly she spun
into usual activity.

Dance to Your Daddy

He had his way with her when she was fourteen.
Some would say there should have been abortion;
to that the parents should have seen.

They did not and *I* am here. Of course there was
a marriage. The parents did see to that.
My mother was fifteen when I was born.

They had a room, one the parents gave them.
For her sake. He never got up in the mornings.
Everyone says I cried a lot. I can

remember screaming, fighting. He hit her.
They tangled on the floor where I was.
I saw everything. They did it all

in front of me. Soon I had a brother. They were
in two rooms then. Her parents gave rent. But he
never got up. Five o'clock in the evening that was

his time. When he left us my mother shook and shook.
She was very thin. Once
he took my brother and me to a place

where a girl was always with him. They did
everything before us. I copied them.
I went up on my brother. They laughed.

But they never got up in the morning. The girl
paid for things. She always had money. She
stuffed soap in my mouth when I cursed.

I cursed the curses he did. After a while
he took us back again to my mother. Men were
often with her. None of them

ever got up in the mornings. Men always
slept. When they finished sleeping
other men came. One man stayed longer

than the others. But not until night
did he get up. Sometimes my mother
took us to school. Now I am a man.

I sleep a lot and take welfare benefit.

Love Me Tender

(with no apologies to Elvis)

How wise Narcissus.
At the early me time I never
loved me—that am the great
I am—that so is everyone—
because the mothers ruled:
'Tis wrong to praise your own.

And that,
as much as anything,
meant me liking that given me.
To make extra sure
the mothers told me every day
about my ugliness.

And so when you and you and you
filled full the adolescent dreams
I worshipped, not you—how not,
since you were deities?
but more, I worshipped me,
imagined exquisite in your godmind.

So much that hungried worship starved
I took it feeding
into every you since then
until of late—it could be light—
or is it age?—
I sometimes feel a care for your own sake.

Library, Section Lit. Crit.

Silence, indeed. And with intent
to paralyse name-dropping makes
great noise. There murders occur.
Books are bloody; predators stalk
the print; crunch, suck to death
what helps to jealous eminence.
Abstractions run amok; abstruse
the blades—the more the fiercer dazzle
death done to the savage flames
on Fame's voracious stone.

> That's it, at once negation and haven:
> College Library, where pulls the pull
> out of the storm to shielded bookish ways.
> One could submit so easily, evade reality;
> could feel how certain natures take one
> sequestered degree after another; could
> explain a Dr Dr Dr I.N.C Green—maybe
> an asphodel grew from his navel;
> perhaps he had a snail on his groin;
> people deserve a refuge; why grudge him?

The Creaking of the Bones

It's a relief, you know, happening this way:
these days I joyfully acclaim my age,
admit the stiffening in the bones. Sometimes
I seize up like an old woman, say, when
I first begin to move having been still
for some time, then I'm locked in my four
joints. (I used to be so limber!)
I do not give too much attention
to the condition, just say hello to it;

give myself a thump, a wallop here and there,
as might a man give a recalcitrant machine
a shake, a jolt without anger, with some affection
even, since it is a machine he has grown somewhat
fond of. Freely now I talk of age who previously
avoided the term: it might put me into focus,
set people, before I was really ready, considering,
speculating. True, though, I always did make
proud point of being exact, giving the racing years

full count. Only it was not too comfortable doing that;
a certain tightness to it; felt easier if people did not
bring the talk around that way. For, you see, life was
flying too fast. You have felt it too, this fear?
It was all whizzing away while always there had been
far too much hard work and no space to be young-silly
in the silly-young time. Therefore to stretch out
youth seemed very necessary just that
I might have time for more experiment.

I had not had full scope to be nonsensical:
children came too fast; I was myself a child
in much that should have been mature
if mother I were. And so, therefore, fear
of tongues and frightened snatch at flying years;
brittle cheer. How ridiculous would be a skittish sheep!
Somehow now much recedes in importance. To
                                        measure
age no longer seems curtailment. A pleased assessment
of the thing is rather what I feel.

Although quiet appraisal sees the seizing bones,
gradual gain of certain ills, and laments indeed
the lessened bounce, the endless surge of energy,
even so, I can celebrate; be glad I am no longer
young, that now my hair goes grey I'll wear it so
(no more the instant dye!); accept my flawed self
as is—it has done some battling—acknowledge where
it failed. Refusing to acclaim victories only, I greet
and even sometimes applaud my uncountable blanks.

Energy of Jura

I am conscious of the mountain,
solid mass, collapsible,
its bulk impresses me to think
of chemists, dissolutions,
nuclear fission, and of mightiness
cosmically unleashed.

Mountain fissioned becomes another
thing and yet remains the same
multiplicity of compacted power
now let differently forth,
its unknowable release
a continuing epic energy.

My mind is mass such
as this—said with due
restraint—I am conscious
of mighty possibilities,
constantly search creation
in my constructive fission.

Blood and Walls

Like what?
—chameleon?—
I change:

when they are there
I grow
so greatly theirs

that their going
is in part
an agony;

reminders
like similar voices,
a laugh, cry,

movement,
a sudden way
the sun slants

in a room
as when they
were there,

starts
that curious reflex
of pain

in the chest
and wetness
in the eyes.

And yet
when they are gone
some long time

I am become
necessarily habituated
to the absence

have attuned
to an existence
without them

have now
become close latched
to a way

of trying
to make the best
of what is there.

I have reached
a fortressed point
where news

of their coming
creates shrinkings,
fears:

my careful
routined structures
will be

wrecked again:
useless quite
my protective plan.

Clearly some decree
requires a willingness
to vulnerability.

Aptitude

There are unprivate times
such as interviews where
you are not much good
at putting on a show and there
they are ranged, the glassy faces,
taking stock of your meagre
surface assortment, your
unlikelihood for this
or this and you feel stripped,
denuded of dignity.

After such times
there is an utter need
to go alone somewhere
far from the obscene
process to which still
quivers your nakedness
as flayed living flesh
and, in the alone, deeply
think into the reaches
of private sureness.

Between You, Me, and the Lamp-Post

Nothing is really private: everyone knows
my business as near as makes no difference;
I know how it goes for you, in my bones

decipher the enigma which is quite simple
really; things add up more or less the same
for you and me. So although pride—or call

it preciousness—prevents my boring you
with matters of multiple intricacy
which weave in and out my life, you

guess, and mostly accurately. And I, too,
am so convinced of replication, you do
not need to fill the picture in. We know

the aberrations—balance being simulated,
greed is plain, easy flesh, cerebral kill.
Maybe sad, my darling neighbour, and yet is quite

right, this pattern of hide and no seek; pure
continuity—everything has happened before
between the beginning and my back door.

Letter to Ireland

Under the butternut trees
envy me in Ontario:
my face is bulbed in mosquito bites
—my eyes, overnight, Eskimo;
I'm Chinese, Japanese;
my eyes are two slits
because yesterday, quite easy
to hazards, I forgot to apply
the repellant and, in a way,
I have slipped identity.

That is good for my Irish soul.
Then continue to envy me:
I write in a moving bowl
with a lid full of holes
and a floor of last year's maple
plus multiple other deciduous leaves
and above me the blue is so coolly
blue because of the green
butternut between this floor
and the noon-sky blaze.

There is furious life in the dead round my feet
including biters who would like my blood
but today my toes wear repellant—
Muskol, brand name, best I am told—
the crawlies reject me. Then further envy me:
the sides of my bowl celebrate and the swishing lid,
these million leaves that, living, weave with breezes

and creatures that fly: the dance in my trees
halleluias the bite in the ground, the future ice
in the wind, the death in the leaf.

Proposal for Magritte

That day in widely gold Touraine we laughed,
how we laughed that day. I remember it now:
our leaden need before it, our blackened hope
that, hopeless, longed for laughter—

bidet plonked beside the sunflowers,
bland enigma
in a landscape empty
but for acres of this high-summer crop.

Our laughing came quick and wild
at such incongruity, too quick,
too wild from the deep,
deep quick of weighted pain,

the cicadas chikking an invading joy
and the sun
insisting golden promise
of the never never.

And we were glad, wild, wildly glad,
in our mad suspending burst, of gold and joke
and dream—or was it some improving farmer
in Touraine?—and pain briefly not.

Bottoms

All right, so you are crusted hard
in burnt gravy and your bottom
I scrub with a wire scraper, while hers
in the TV corner flashes a shiny bikini
to sell a cocktail, a car or again
—with a number of other rumps—
capers in stretch denim to promote
a line in jeans.

Old saucepan that I clean,
everything is a possible
subject for a poem.

And curiously, scraping yours, I get
a flash of other bottoms in some ways
like yours but different: older,
more battered; younger also—
those of babies afflicted with diarrhoea
that I have treated with
hygiene and affection
through gritted teeth.

And there, facing me, hung on a hook,
the plastic bum of a wash-up basin,
new, and still of untried character.

What about the backsides
of buses,
sixth or ninth in a row
slizzing past
with a contemptuous fart

diminishing the air
leaving me stranded
with whatever load?

And yet again
the posterior of a thought
I do not care to face.

I know a lot about backsides:
every day, many times a day,
I am presented with their lineaments
not needing to see–
I know too well the geography.
And therefore let us celebrate:
Halleluia!

Brian Boru and Aurora

They told me of the brutal Danes
—I was five years old—
how they came for centuries

to burn, pillage, butcher ...
In Clontarf there was Broder,
Brian Boru cleft, blood and slaughter.

I was not too clear on the history
but I saw raw bodies
and terrible savagery.

Funny, helping mother, when I was five—
worked Broder—never left the country—
Broderick, still strong, in spite of Clontarf,

mother's help, jibing at her own Broderick name.
My mother, too, was clear that she, herself,
had Danes in her frame:

her eyes were snowfield blue, all
thistle-fluff her young light hair,
and the men in her clan very tall.

Now I am in Denmark, every northern door
is a broad yes, tall Danes greet honestly;
I feel an empathy as nowhere, quite, before.

Pleasant to ears gone vicious
with Irish bitching
are Danish women, clever, yet exuding no malice.

Too well I know—cannot be fool—
the universal bitch, the he-she,
the you-me, the real eternal;

but I eat, my time being short with Danes,
their uncommon sun, store in one week
warmth against advancing Dublin ice.

Part IV

from *Let Live*, 1990

Let Live

They had discovered this bit of Ireland
and, although shrewd, adored; it was
their Grail, their Ganges, hill of Olivet,
somehow idealised focus
of their travelled hearts,
still searching
from inside
their earthwatch shapes
—no meat, no nicotine—
of alternative culture.

They had searched the four ends
until finding this late scrag of rock
and heather where they settled.
The knowing locals savoured their oddness
—blow-ins, better than TV, three dimensional;
their sweat lodges and naked capering
under the moon were marked with prurient
spasm from behind furze bushes,
became the stuff of slippery yarns.

However, since astuteness
was on both sides,
the blow-ins took
the local measure
and laughed
at their own imagined ridicule:
they envisaged a permanent sojourn
and laughing
was to mutual advantage.

They asked me what do poets
carry in their pockets.
I said
I could answer only for myself:
this time of year it was bound
to be lavender heads whereupon
I showed them. They were pleased
and I was invited to drink lassi
and later furze blossom wine.

The Learning Process

We learned new things from him,
our travelling companion,
a man so previously engrossed
in very private occupation
he had not learned
what everyone surely knew
through daily osmosis:
he therefore remarked with wonder
at the carrying of a new baby
in a frontal sling by its father;
the sworn-original type of pancake place
so general these days;
the folding of a napkin
around a wine neck to prevent drips.

When challenged on this last
ridiculous ignorance, he said,
a shade defensively,
that in his background
wine would not anyhow have been
'house' wine and waiters would
anyhow have poured it for one,
the napkin being rather
over their arm than around
the bottle-neck.
There was an adjustment
of holiday protective covering
as we turned to smile, revised,
our mocking mutual armour.

Peanut Queenie

When you go a very long journey
with friends in their car
it is necessary to play your part.
You must bring supplies
to keep things going:
small talk, some of them,
the appropriate noises
at novel sights in the landscape,
a constant level of enthusiasm
for conveniences made available,
the obligingness or otherwise
of the weather et cetera, et cetera.

It is a very tiring necessity,
this furnishing of supplies.
At the end there is considerable comfort
in not having to exclaim about it all,
the endless beauty of the scenery
having become merciless.
After seven hundred miles
and mannerly enquiry,
they tune into pop radio
and contrary to earlier convictions
you find you love Peanut Queenie,
The Queen of the Dancing Floor.

Unapprehended

Dark song arose,
Black
out of the black clefts
borne out of the rocks upheaved jag.

Primeval, before any knowing,
holding the balancing stars;
out beyond the rim of things,
beat dark song.

Old song.
Before ever was life
was the beat of song,
first beat, of the life thought.

Strong heavy beat,
to shatter through my flesh now
and shake to wrenching sobs
what holds the shape of me.

Beat on beat
where is life is beat
of old sadness going back
and back and then on and on.

Forces—North Kerry

Curlew-cry:
some old sorrow
always rises
out of the wistful earth
at the curlew's passing.
Sad power of old mountains.
Ancient sorrow swells
on the lonesome dark,
clouds folding down
by the lone lake side.
Old pain rears
out of the pagan past
and I am cleft
with sweep of pagan sorrow
that is such pristine joy
by the lake's lone side
when the curlew cries.

To My Mother

Just before sleep last night
I remembered.

Little woman
bearer of big men.

And before sleep
with knowledge near to tears
I knew again your fight.

Saw
the tired body sit so straight
while hands went on mending
into the late night.

Saw
the weary head
yet firm because of the strong will
bend over books that had to be known
for school on the morrow.

Knew
With surer knowing
your unflinching wrestle
with careful spending
of the much-earned wage.

Remembered
the special care of little things:
for grace of summer curtains
or flowers gathered in still busy

interlude from imperative chores—
remembered, now humble, and with praise.

Remembered too
the slight body in vivid action
against encroaching weeds,
impotently militant against
frequent defeat by horse and cow
in your limited domain.

As mothers live, and see
their children pass from them,
unknowing, I knew your grief.

And now
on hearing great music
tears run and run
for this and this.

I have lived these years
and know but now
pain of mothers
amid their children's going.

Gaspé to Ottawa

That was Wednesday and after days
we were coming back,
the evening sending up its warmed haze.
On our right a track,

a brittle sweep of acceptable gold:
the sun across that river
wide as a sea. I, queerly sad,
felt, improbably, a leaving. Goodbye river.

Vast, old, so old; it said what it said:
I would have liked a long flow
of the impossible—our driver sped—
to know what, to know.

Our driver sped. I was thinking
—illogical knife—Is it the last time
for this and this (you sleeping)
the last time?

And then your sleeping was a threat.
Unimpressed, but plainly vulnerable you were,
not having been able to simulate
a constitution remaining in interested gear.

Drained by such persistent panorama,
you did not see nor care
that we were coming back this different way
with, on our right, the splendid water.

Following us always on the left, repeated flight
of silver things, flashing an imaginable history—
silo towers, thin spires, new roofs—their light
the aluminium glint of Canada.

Its dark force of northern heights was cobwebbed later
and queerly sad. The river had said
what it said. I, remembering now, know nothing better:
not this nor this … and now you are dead.

However Long that Dark

(from the original Irish, 1989:
Dá Fhad an Oíche)

Today will be black night
and pain will spear each pulse—
I know it;
the dark tunnel on and on—
this I understand;
life that is as death for you—
I feel it.
I know, understand, feel,
because it was for me
a like stretch of time;
by this I am marked
so that now with utter sureness
I can urge you, beloved human,
to search out your courage;
even if the bitter stone
in your chest is, you think,
for ever
and you can take no more,
hold fast, hold fast:
that stone will melt,
the tunnel will become
a flow of discovery
and it will be again morning—
I have seen it.

Progenitors

For some unknowable reason
memory is at its unpredictable doings
and you are suddenly there
in my crowded morning.

On this capricious summer day
whys and whys in new questionings
query unaccountably in my head.
I didn't really know you, Dad.

Just loved you. I think: soon
I will reach the span of your years
and how unknown, in sum, you were,
I am, is anyone, at the end.

We bury, burn, turn from cemeteries,
crematoria, resuming the necessary banal
but you, all the rated dead, eclipsed
by clay, waters, do not die.

Irrelevant to our usual capers, you are
suddenly back: a look, a quality, the answers
still missing and, in the self-important busyness,
somewhere a cry, a long longing.

The Giant's Causeway

Where the giant was we too are here,
that mighty he, sprung huge from
the imagination of emergent men
to signify a yearned-for power.

They, longing to master the deadly threat
of elements, beasts, other men, saw
the causeway as his stepping-stones athwart
a swallowing sea, to him their shallow feat.

With new views now, we see molten power
cooled to enduring prism: it witnesses to giant
still, just barely held beneath the front,
the shell of earth, daily face of me and you.

Bloody Foreland

Sponsored meagrely they came, eager,
the London students, extending to all deprived
their working fluency. After Bogside, Derry,
they came to view how Donegal contrived
—in their hired mini-bus—with kelp and dole
and fish and grants, old settlements redone
to modern demands: stuff for the whole
diploma thesis. In the parlour fun

with the foxy priest, whiskey and lulling turf:
nothing deprived. Before dusk they bunch
by Bloody Foreland, squaring to the rough
change, taking photos: themselves against March
sky, the furious cliffs, the madder seas.
The Land of Youth, one says, breathing the storm
on top of whiskey. The white mares
gallop endlessly to the shore.

Achill

City people get lost here, drawn
into measureless seductions;
Mweenaun twilight takes their senses,
the slender magnet of a young moon;

they even leave a lover's bed to watch
the dark turn day above Slieve More.
Light is in command here, dictating behaviour
to holiday folk, ruling deluge,

determining the turn of shark and seal,
the hours of gale. But this place
of light and spell does not really grace,
compelled away in cold centuries people,

those who came to live. It lures
assured in ageless age, there it
waits, laughing its light,
avenging on later men its scars.

Beara Peninsula

There we are. See us now, high. Shock:
we cling, clutch in the bladed furze.
Fastnet far, flung on a foaming rock
in a wide empty water—a kind of fear:

that foaming band pulls down—
look up! that empty sea
charged full from wind and moon
compels our eye—oh up! look up!

What are we doing here with our mouths
laughing like the yellow gorse,
our skin in ecstasy as heather curves
to the windy clouds?

Barrow Estuary

Talk about the Barrow Estuary
and I'll see Strongbow and McMurrough's Aoife
wedded in the streets flowing blood.
For so to our child-mind it was told.

We carried Norman genes, loved atrocities,
while frightened at our leaping brutal relish.
Much older, with approved manners, we were guests
in a stronghold on those easy Barrow swards.

Travel firms pronounced it the sunniest corner
and though crops swelled on this alluvial cover
and Dermot, Strongbow, Aoife fed less imagination,
Bretons cycle past, hawking strings of onions.

Dublin Bay

A good time to come is January:
there is a geranium sky behind Longford Terrace,
a black pine gone mad between chimneys,
from where you stand by the abandoned soap factory.

Turn right: the town is walled in mist;
no twentieth century, but hard, sure,
the winter rip of Vikings, tearing dire
by Howth, fogged also, yet solid, fast.

You are back where Brian seemed holy,
praying in Clontarf. There are no bulls either
nor the strewn excesses of a modern summer
at Seapoint. Only the cormorants, happy,

and the ceaseless pagan sea; you climb
as do two or three others, each alone
trudging towards that queer geranium zone ...
January, there, is a good time.

Henrietta, Caleb and Issue

A squat shape, Hetty,
nourished on a budgeted supply
of Wicklow stew
which was, depending on your view
helped out with sausages
or embellished with them;
not browned first
—a waste of fuel, that—
they remained pig pink and swam.

Salt of the earth, her tight community,
all solid principles seriously applied, in poor supply
joy—laughing, a serious matter also its roots:
they had to be solidly held, no bubbling hoots
nor unhinged yells, no mad flight of the ridiculous.
laughter, in fact, required a licence:
Limited duration, restricted areas
only, controlled pitch and volume,
salvation likeliest reached with a frown.

Over forty, Hetty was twenty years a member when
Caleb—newcome from Wales, a widower then—
joined the Walkers' Club. After
careful months, they walked to the sensible altar.
Serious gardeners, they had still time for one fruit;
indeed two grew; each, in time, and nourished
on salutary economy, took prizes, flourished.
Hetty squatly took their praise as her meed,
Caleb's earnest smile said the Lord saw them good.

So Caleb took early retirement, brought
them all to Calgary where had been wrought
a century's solid network of the faith.
Unerringly, Hetty had planned their path
from Wicklow, now established principled contacts
as was her way; sustaining stew continued
and other right practices; joy maintained
a distance; according to foreseeable manoeuvres
she would shortly implement marriages.

However
the prize fruit, earners
of their own
good money,
set up
individual abodes;
then, madly laughing, rose
to proceed with explorations
of unlimited dimensions.

September Song

One of these days I'll take myself in hand, get
some money together and buy a small car that works.
I'm fed up with the discouraging old carcass
crouched by the pavement, its every joint
and muscle geared to misbehave or block—
a surly clogged-up lump, intractable. It is
too like myself. I need a car that will encourage me,
that will, for instance, keep the rear-view mirror
steady and operate with soothing reflex
as do the cars of friends who give me
lifts. I'd like a realistic backward measure:
I tend to put a lot down to the stiffness in my neck.

I'll get my eyes seen to before that.
There are things they can do these days:
there's that laser operation—
gives you the shivers when you think of it
although I know a teenager who swears
by it. Her father had money and didn't shun
the price. She said, securely,
'My Daddy loves me'. I have
no Dad and spare money never a bit
but I'll get it together somehow for he's costly,
this tricky eye-man, a defected Slav—
I tend to put a lot down to poor sight.

And in my new car that works,
giving me a true rear view,
maybe I could venture alone this time to Cahirciveen,
attempt long slow ways to Vienna or Aix-
en-Provence, along boreens—they don't know

that word in Europe—for, even
with my new laser view forward
and my steady rear-view mirror, I'll still
need boosting, will wish to keep clear
of all carrier trucks that brute the ground,
ten-wheel furies to suck you in their violent pull
and, like some memories, blast a courage mostly fear.

Hola Verdad!

There is something soothing to the ego
in having before you the puzzled look
of a foreign student eager to learn your lingo:
there you are, for once at a clear advantage,
in entire command, with valuable assets.

You make full use of such a situation;
you are not, understood, a teacher, rather
a creature with pleasanter connotations,
a free giver, with (you fancy) impeccable
enunciation *and* in a social context.

Granted the social aspect is a little awry,
for you articulate a pace unnatural to your
volatile disposition which, many times, has had
you in jeopardy but then, for that very reason,
the easing of speed is mutually beneficial.

You expound—just a trifle, too much abstraction
being irrelevant and you are, anyway, somewhat
tongue-in-cheek; however, to pontificate thus
minimally, is emollient; you are so unquestionably,
now, the authority: who is to gainsay you?

Enjoying the safety, you proceed, invent,
but do not pretend a lot, just stretch sometimes
the boundaries of your travels, amplify adventures:
you allow yourself such latitude as pardonable
exercise in verbs, especially those hanging on if.

Mainly you stay with objects round about
or those likeliest to be encompassed
in the student's day; you give him valuable
conversational English and warm to the zeal
with which he always puts anxious jottings

in his inside zipped pocket; you like
to imagine him later perusing them
in compliment to your precious bestowal,
committing them to permanence, that is to say
a notebook or, highest value, memory.

You are making your mark,
are impressing as more than adequate,
are, indeed, highly regarded
—all amusing ballast against
your inner facts of self-encounter.

'Counterrevolution'

In remote Trassac, first day,
you stretch your city shape
under the great light
that arcs south
above the massive limestone hang:
a little healing promises your skin
and stays, encouraging hips, knees.

Four successive days you amble
to the hamlet Marcilhac-sur-Célé;
going to buy your baguette,
you find the boulangerie
already almost bare
for the buying is always early
and you are holiday late.

You might meet no-one, see
only the deaf mute, guardian
of the bells, taking it easy
since no tourists; old abbey
walls warm benign in the sun,
grudges against that Amadour
long lapsed to mere anecdote.

For four sequestered days
no TV, cassettes, radio,
no news, no outside world;
you have been free
from urban filth, thriven
in this rare peace, green air,
profusion of wild buds.

After twilight
down by the Célé,
the night birds pipe,
each time a single note,
the cliffs holding the pure sound.
On the third night
the moon comes almost full.

Today, paying for your wine,
you include La Dépêche
from the pile: local fun, you think,
pétanque and little fêtes—
and then you see
the murdered young, the riddled dead
in Tiananmen Square.

Yellow Joke

I have a great liking
for the ridiculous,
the way it makes
a fatal hole in solemnity,
letting in
the light of laughter.

The sky cracked
and there was a huge laughing.

Lightning ridicules, splitting
pompous clouds, rending
their bloated threat
to the splendid mockery
of thunder,
the elemental hilarity
of crazy rain.

Let us enjoy the banana skin
bringing dictators to the ground.

Thomas Mann Country

You can walk the canal path from Lubeck
to Hamburg and with you all the way go
great poplars; the life span of their kind
I do not know but their giant rustling
seems as news of centuries; the water
carries Baltic lore under their imaged shapes.

In Thomas Mann country trees flourish to rich height,
their drink the lakes, their flood alluvium of aeons;
their multiplicity of birds seem not to sleep in June
for, wakeful,you hear them cheep the short night,
chutter until quick light when, transcendently,
they celebrate—an energy of joy, unique.

A generous place: portions your plate.
In the Saturday square a travelling troupe mimes
a parody to medieval instruments. Hard by,summer
of smoked sausages, a row of mustards—all hot
in a cool June. You eat yours funnelled in bread
by the cathedral wall, decide to move southwards.

The canal stems villages, buildings flower either side;
gardens replicate symmetry, the irregular has, it seems,
no countenance in this land: dawn hears workers
on their scheduled way to responsible field, city hours.
Plan, produce: a positive programme. Sunday,
in a burst of shurbs, the timbered tiny church
                                        pulled by its age,

you enter, notice dates; variety of ancient patterning
on wood, hand-painted; the brushed and tailored
                                        gathering.
You stay to hear. Later, in your white bed, wakeful
as the night-long chutter in the trees, you keep seeing
that savage passion of the preacher who flashed his fist
and yelled at the unanswering assembled faces.

Bald

To endow my emulative compositions
with a global dimension
a universally concerned aura—indeed,
maybe, even extraterrestrial, since
all that space is for agonising—
I have a list of things to put in poems:
you get nowhere these days in the arts
unless you ring convincing
in your urgency to radical reform,
to far-reaching influence.

And yet today, I feel myself
primarily moved to write about
those balding heads.
Not on the list but
for years they have disturbed me
and I have kept reminding myself—
and then forgetting—to put reactions,
nicely crafted, on paper
with just the degree of detachment
to win critical approval.

I am always troubled to see
those unhappy strands compelled
to freakish length athwart the bone, coerced
from their natural home, still-active border
above the ear, or even—unhappier yet—
dislocated from the innate downward drift
of poll and dragged across the scalp,
itself an honourable, often very handsome

manifestation but now mocked, diminished
by such grotesque overlay.

I applaud the exposed dome,
give it special praise,
find it has a dignity; enhances presence;
there are those we know who carry it so.
They have, of course, other baldnesses
they cover as mine do I who wear my thatch
with a difference—that's why I now suggest
to all of us baldies a hanging on to courage,
letting the hair fall as it may: possibly
this rings sufficiently global for today?

Liberté, Dublin '89

Rare summer, the guards are down.
There are riots of enthusiastic flesh.
Previously held unsuitabilities appear,
uncensured, all judgement waived. Standards
swivel, allowing general amnesty. Fat secrets
roll about, become confessional. The bus stop
sees the back of truth much wrinkled
in a low-cut scrap. Intemperate shorts
walk dogs and juiceless flanks. Long teeth
go shopping, wearing minimum, easy
in the flop of accumulated mounds. There is
a large relief at relinquished camouflage.
The beach supports alignments, disrobings
alongside total strangers, proximities
scandalous in a winter context. Anywhere,
quite likely, a divinely vulgar statement
of blemished flesh, no longer cowering,
rejected, attempting apologetic disguise.
Meanwhile, around some ruling bodies
there remains the customary fog
and the letter-box, each post, canvasses
for the Senate. Later, there will be
revisions, the knives freshly in place.

Summer Seine

On the shrubby end of Ile Saint Louis
you may sit, absorbing. You are
in that suspended solitariness that is
for good and bad in great cities; there,
ignored, ignoring, private, exclusive until—
it is about three-thirty. Friday afternoon—
the increasing madness beyond each river wall
presses in, hearing suffers a lunatic invasion:
the ravening engines attacking ears plus
the obligatory weekend out of town.
Late Sunday, unnourished, will witness
their peevish, nosetail, crawled return.
Watching the easy nod of leaves
in the light river winds,
you re-achieve a thankful deafness,
a relative belief in the good of islands.

Making

The chart showed the sun in one
of its cyclic passions, flinging off
fireballs, flares; against it, mere dot,
the earth, chart black, 'Extinction',

they said, 'A new hell, it will get us all.'
'Not you,' we said, 'not you nor us; we will
all be long gone in our own brand of scorch:
rivalries, cliques, coteries.'

Meanwhile, the deathless lust to make is full:
see how she, a throbbing twelve, awaits
the monthly seal of power, her small buds
athrust, her lips a knowing scarlet call.

See how he, any age, always hopeful organ,
snuffs, advances, stirrings in the groin.
It will be, despite annihilations: in fine,
because of them? O magnificent why!

Pram

Poor as poor, we bought the pram
on the never never—there was
no other way. The cheapest there,
an excuse of a thing. I cannot recall
exact cost, I think twelve quid, a huge
sum for us then and, of course, the interest
brought it up more; always, everything
we had to pay was too much—even so,
sometimes we took a guilty coffee
and a cake at the Roman Cafe.
　　About the pram, they
stamped the instalment book—my name,
the mother, more appropriate—each week
but the father paid: we were pledged
partners, did things together. I
hadn't a sou—reasons for that too.
He paid strictly except
the last bit, the child a year, pram
already wrecking.
There came
　　a threatening letter:
certain unavoidable consequences in the event
of nonpayment—a fine or prison. I see my
big mouth, loud, to friends declaring
I would go to gaol. To me, I was
spirited, vocal, making a case against
shoddy goods, usury. I knew, too,
appetite for experience, for keeping up
the fight against background where gaol
was a disgrace—I hadn't thought it out.

        The friends who had
little, were generous: they paid. I must
reassert I was in full earnest but they
said it would harm the child,
also the father in his
skimpy vital job. It would
harm them, too, standing by
and letting happen.
A mean thought that;
it came later.
        I have since
harmed the child
and the child
and the child …
there have been so many. And—
is it worse?—
about keeping
my mouth shut,
I have learned much.

Part V

New Poems

Woad and Olive

Boadicea came to see me.
She had been down our south
and across to our west.
She said she had wanted
to move amongst the people,
get to know the real thing.

She had been very happily treated,
taken with the beauty of our country,
had met many people, was surprised
to find forty percent of these to be
of recent English and continental origin.

There had been, it appeared,
a process of peaceful acquisition.
It was nourishing, said she, to see
what seemed such harmonious coexistence.
After her long centuries' sojourn
in another realm, she
had come to the conclusion
that a just plurality
was a desirable modus vivendi.

I told Boadicea that in my youth
my older sibling bashed my face
and walked on my guts.
I did not stay lying down
but constantly worked out
strategies of revenge.
This kind of thing had gone on for years.

Our family was no different from others.
In a neighbouring bog was found a woman
done to death in a most brutal fashion
with a digging spade. Of her husband
and brother who had lived with them
there was no trace. A wife had spat
on a dying mate, speeding him on.

All these matters had given me
unsettling views on the ferocities
possible in close relationships.

I had wanted my older sibling
to say 'Well done, old girl!'
as brothers said in *Girls Own Paper*
where they also opened doors for sisters
and gave them birthday presents.

When I shot up a tree
and slithered lightning
down again,
the Rector's son said,
'Old girl, well done.'
Protestants were nicer,
I told my mother then.

I could make no sense
of the human race, I said
to Boadicea. She replied
she understood; she had noticed,
too, that we had woad in common—
I was wearing my purple shot with blue—
but hers she wore no longer.

When she left
there were no blades
in her chariot wheels
and she handed me
an olive branch.

Feet

Whole histories get divulged
in buses
between stop and stop.

A heavy woman said she slipped
on the supermarket floor—
supergloss, said she, heavily—
and her foot folded up like a sandwich.
You gotta keep goin', she said.

A man gave me his seat, only,
he said, because he hoped I would
take him on my lap. Clutching the bar,
he smiled big, a shiny wet,
a ridge of ochred teeth.

When he got off I saw,
—not until then—
his shrivelled limp
through the gate of the Institution.

Thinking of Kevin McAleer, Derrida and Hogan Shea

I'd like to see a Kevin McAleer
on Derrida. There is an unthinkable
tonnage of paper recording the turnout
of words required by the system
to gain this and that advantage—
letters after the name, tenure,
head of the faculty, head of
thinking and so on. Think
of the phoniness. Come on Kevin.

In our district dictionary meanings
got reversed in the local vocabulary:
a ditch was a dyke, a dyke a ditch.
We understood one another perfectly
as far as that went. There was
a simplicity complex to the outsider.

You who are on the inside
will understand me when I say
Hogan Shea stuck his head
under the single strand of wire
paled on a ditch. He did this
as an ostrich sticks his head
in sand, believing his invisibility.

No-one knew why Hogan Shea wished
to be invisible but we knew his rap
on the pane for food. Having placed
it, we never once saw him take it.

But he was sometimes visible
scuttling over fields, a clotted
thing of coats and coats and hair
and hair who slept with animals.

Now, washing at night and again
in the morning, being hygienic
about expensive trivia like lenses
and dental plates, checking off
the metaphorical egg on the frontage
of my disabled son, polishing up,
brushing down, making ready
the positive facade
to salute the gimlet public,

and all this day after day after day,
I think of Derrida, of Hogan Shea,
the comfort in layered skins of unwashed
coats, of nested hair, of becoming invisible
with my head under a single strand
of wire on the ditch, of a long sleep
free of angel dust, warmed
by the breath of a few authentic cows.

Further Matter for Magritte

As we tear along towards Banteer
a dandelion seed on a current of air
that brings it from the green
and white and yellow of spring
along the Kerry line
through a narrow aperture
above the synthetic surfaces
of the CIE carriage
to daintily float
as moves the breeze,
settles gently in the ear
of an aging man
with painful hump
and a certain effluvium,
lugging a case wherein,
doubtless, are artefacts
of his somewhere sojourn.

What if seed germinate
in the plentiful aural alluvium
so that, later summer, the ear
will flower a brave paean
of fructification?
More style in that surely than
in a scrubbed hygiene
of unlovely purpling whorls?

My Darling Women

It's just a way of speaking—don't take
the darling too seriously.

Somewhat affected
you might think,
this *façon de parler*
but now that I look at it
it just happened
not a conscious process.

We pick things up, don't we,
as we move along; they accrue without
our noticing, adhere to the moving pile—
best see them positively, as possible alluvium:
they can have their enriching fun, allow us
some salutary self-ridicule,
Narcissus dying laughing.

Ultimately perhaps it's all best seen
as comedy, final balance to daily
senseless waste of bodies, efforts,
artefacts like temples, towers of rule.

Anyhow for the present here we are,
the women, in our new way, determined
on information and leaving the country
whenever.
There at the top, our admirable Head
of State—I cherish a letter from her—
on the offing a female Taoiseach.
I'm counting up.

The other night ranged at the long table
were the strong women, insisting
our rights before Maastricht. Listeners
thronged. 'It was hard,' the widow next me
said. Drunkard husband. She'd stitched
to school their spawn of eight, all
good jobs now. 'Tis the women do it,'
she said, 'But my time was brainwashed.
Those up there are great, claiming the claims.'

I try to keep abreast, stroke every night
my PCW on the shoulder, say, Dear Amstrad,
continue to be my friend. I switch it on—
neuter, notice—to make sure; its answering
click leaves me happy. No insertion. Just
checking. Goodnight Amstrad. I switch it off,
hope for co-operation. It needs its frequent
frisson, my nervous touch; can sulk, require
long bouts in the parlours if I neglect.

I'm counting up, to enumerate being more
than ever a required activity. I still
do it quite a lot on my fingers, Amstrad
notwithstanding: it's good sometimes
to recognise limitations. There was
Alma Mahler, she did not face the facts;
got her mirror wrong; encased in
mountainous well-aged flesh, she roused
only revulsion in the young Canetti.

And after Maastricht, there we were
in the future, free to choose—
information, travel, matters of the womb.
We had worked hard at it, hadn't we?
Sorority. For presuming hussies who
warbled into rehearsal, divas—
Searc Yeelis, Cailleach Nimhe and others—
still showed thumbs down. In some respects,
matters of ego for example, nothing had changed.

Fifty Years On

You were right you know,
I got him wrong.
He was none, you said,
of the things I saw in him.

You'll remember my poem: I called it
'Twenty-five'—his age—it's in
the 'Early' section. Yes, you were
right: after fifty years I've met him again.

No 'pale wistful boy'
no 'naked soul' in the eyes.
One of the practised diplomats,
the clever stare requisite.

No 'searching, seeking humanity'.
he had slimed through
all the sticky channels
to that post of seal and style.

As 'lonely searcher
under the wetness of mists
blown from shore mountains'
I fancifully saw him.

It strikes me now
his shakes, pouchy eyes,
liverish yellow, testify
to saturation of another sort.

Of course I was romantic then:
there were sheep and goats.
I'm still shortsighted—always
those saddling spectacles, but
a thing or two I see more clearly
and lately I walk a bit better—
my two sheep hooves, two goat.

Sour

I saw Benjie's phiz on the page last night
a print from days long gone.
They'd plenty others so whose was the thought?
Theirs, or his out of pride?

You'd think by now he'd be well past that
and accept his years with grace.
But true that age can lust for young meat,
urge a man to repeated chase.

Next week on the air he'll host the show
do it well, with panache, it's his style;
they'll love him, they'll clap him, they always do,
that print could have stayed in the file.

A wheeler dealer, said someone close,
a colleague he'd left in the lurch
as onward and upward he spun and rose,
self-interest his chapel and church.

Not once this year last year or before
did he ask me or wink or say come;
my timber was never the sort for his spoke;
I'm sucking these grapes here: have some?

Tournesol

It has lost all juices now,
that one leg, gently grey,
that hangs these years level
with my bedroom door,
its ankle spancelled
to a high hook with a ribbon
that has lost first yellow.

When we used the picnic knife
to slice it—leaves, enduring
face—from such southern light,
we asked it to forgive: it had
witnessed a day particular in rift
and bond, it and the thousand
others in that square bright acre,
one of the countless such across
a sunflowering France.

We said we needed all
it signified
for our ties and light
into a dark future.

On our return I hung it where
there were enterings and leavings.
The future has gone into the past.
He, merged in that, had to leave.

They would have mown it anyhow,
crushed to its last vestige.
I have seen what happens in September.

With us it had six years.
When he had to go, it stayed
this further six. Mummified,
true, but always functioning.
In passing, I frequently touch
its faithful length, sometimes
stoop to talk to its still-wide
face turned, as ever since its
first witnessing, to the ground.
Now and then I take a dwindled seed,
chew, release the quick knife
from its memoried dusty case,
the blade, the irretrievable joy.

Masochist

I despise banalities, utter them
all the time, wish for that withdrawn
silence of the egghead which whams viciously,
freezes blisters on your mucus membrane.

However, this was a bank clerk.
His thumbnail on my withdrawal slip
—a piddling sum, twenty quid—
was square trimmed and whitewash white.

Mine was black with dandelion iron.
I had the strongest push to say
I see you don't do any gardening,
despised such rot, gave it instant way.

Through his bank clerk's glasses
a fleck of indulgence reduced it
further: currency of the banal,
twenty quid my limit.

Blarney Machree

My neighbour and I rush
into mutually laudatory remarks.
I tell her I like her dress.
I don't. She says

You're looking great,
she is looking at the cold sore
that's started up on
the way in to my nostril.

You're working all out, I say,
killing yourself, you ought to be
takin' it easy, takin', it slow,
like Bob Marley.

Ah I'm not a patch on you,
says she, look at the way
you've been turning the place
inside out.

I have too but not the way she means.
I now have a device on my door to keep
a check on things. It doesn't work.
As for my tongue … ah well …

In my youth he sang
Once again I'll say I love you
with your bonnie eyes of blue,
little sweetheart of the meadows

etcetera.
I weighed twelve stone
and my eyes were stony green.

Curves

1

Nature moves in curves. I see
no straight lines in it anywhere.
Now my friend upstairs, the scientist,
sees differently. Yet his rigid route
between point and point seems to me
no nearer the ultimate mark.
Well, who can tell it anyway?
Besides, he himself lives curved:
his appetite makes dewlaps, bellygross.

You have only to observe the leaders
to tell they cannot tell.

As for me, I am always jigsaw.
No matter how I attempt to chart
a rational plan in the manner
of approved minds, wayward stuff
persists, intrudes. Angles I carefully
calculate and arrange give way,
become open ground which allows,
from some crowded source, invasion
of shapes claiming their parade.

Given head, they can rush, become a tumult
which must thresh its arbitrary course.
When it settles, I can go around—
it takes much time—fitting convex to concave,
create design. It takes much time.

Even then the picture may still be
open-edged, refusing the confines of frame
as if ready for a possibility
of continuing loops … continuing.

2

Grown-ups changed their talk
if they noticed me.
I hungered for their secrets.

Around the burning mugs their nails
were black with our peaty earth,
the two men in from the field.
She could swallow both, her hollows
ready, the girl who placed their bread.
Plenty of that. Hungry, she stood.
They sat. Talk at least
they would feed her.

I, too, with my cravings, waited.
But they knew
my shrunken corner crouch.
They changed the talk
it would have been
had they not seen me,
gathered small
under listening eyelids.

Bloodsuckers in a drain
clamped
on a drowning weasel,
of this they spoke,

their chunks
of sideways bread hinting
a cruel food, the girl empty,
I waiting.

Leeches.
They terrified me.
More than any other
unexplained dark life,
I abhorred
their imagined curves
blind upon my early flesh,
relentless violation.

February '92

—and so, his left hand
in desk drab pocket,
his right had—no overcoat—
the walkie-talkie to his ear.

He was walking down Maretimo
Road, listening to the voices
of duty, his bureau feet
astray in the flirting buds.

They're really out of synch,
post office girl said, passed
the change, meant the seasons.
Old customer said True, stuck

trembling stamps; upside down
winter had borne her
alive to hobble pleasure,
post in the sungreen box.

Flying Visit, Finland '92

Not seen in living memory: begging bowls
in the street. Before going I had read of it.
Once there, I am told the begging march
with bowls and banging spoons was to protest
radical attention. They had had
a vaunted rate of work, only one without
per hundred. In a single year one became
thirteen, evil number, symbol of imminence
unless … things had slumped disturbingly.

In my flying visit I was truly received,
register only positive aspects.
A deliberating people, sparse, wedged between
big powers, yet, in their race and tongue,
impressively singular, of uncharted beginnings.
Tenaciously, they have endured, preserved
their worthy pride, power of identity;
are, withal, now a majority agreed to risk
a destiny in this fluctuant new Europe.

They seem to soak up languages as sponge liquid:
give them one year where English is first tongue,
their school basics turn a free vernacular;
anywhere—could be washroom, street, academe—
I find a mutual speech; in the Archives, intense
young Finn surprises me with fruit of his
Galway year: we have an hour's rapport in Irish.
Why is it our fourteen years' or so pursuance
mostly fails to nurture such a blossoming?

A balance-seeking land: nine months' snow
but comforting houses. When, my key lost,
I called out the caretaker, she—motherly
past midnight, dressing gown, wallops
of sleet—simply hugged quiet my deep
apologies. I delight in grace of general
good manners, rare in our time, suspend
sharp edges, blunt into the pleasures
of such emollient discipline and warmth.

Surviving, Helsinki, Turku '92

In predatory bent from a bleak
Baltic, the flocking gulls,
powered by their fierce
beat to live, mangle the air
above the well-fed stalls
at buying time,

do not alight,
await the less-peopled hour
when stands are closed
and scraps, in spite
of sellers' Nordic care,
may lie about.

However urged by savage maw,
the gulls hold back, do not
trust these providing people
who shout little and walk
collectedly. Gulls
have learned: stronger

than even hunger, a born store
fuels their ravening being,
alerts to all moving animals,
warns of the essential—
a wait, albeit furious
towards pleasure delayed.

The careful folk themselves,
on the cold edge of a continent,
consider before speech, do not rush

to answer: perhaps they prize
such chosen space, its distancing,
after years' devouring dominance.

Brim

Winter men
wear hats in Helsinki,
in Turku
they do too:

Al Capone hats
or those of lover-boys
who lit cigarettes
in murky nooks

on the black and white
screen, spelling
sophistication,
urban romance,

to my ignorant island
youth. Am I
wiser now: long tooth
worn bones, white hair?

Odd, that inside this
costly seen-it-all,
stirs the ghost of a girl,
eager, at the tilt of a hat.

Circling

Sunflowers pursue me—
that, and say hello
in the most unlikely places,
for example, the Finno-Ugrian Centre.

In this land of still-iced lakes,
unmarked snow, Helsinki cherishes,
within ponderous walls conserves,
evidence of a related culture, in crisis.

There sunflowers speak: handcrafted,
they witness from spaces, pages, weaves;
defy annihilation, symbolise a tough
dark heart, encircling light that holds.

At the hotel I finish breakfast—
grapes, soft cheese, tiny cinnamon rolls—
glance about and in the cleverly wrought
window-glass find sunflowers patterning.

For me, they go back and back:
1975 they were *'Subject for Magritte'*,
'bidet in the sunflowers'.
It is now April 1992.

In the bus from Turku, soon to stop,
my literary colleague, duly hirsute,
snores a last few through
his indigenous crop.

Soon now the airport.
We return to roots: he south,
I, where these years by my door
hangs upside down a sunflower.

Points of View

We traded advice—remember? at the bureau
de change: I suggested you be kind to your
mother, keep off the drink. 'Watch out,'
you said, 'for the spitting blondes, those

six-foot goddesses coming towards you,
rivetting you with their long grace.
And what do they do a foot or less,
in front of you but hawk and spit—

never saw the like!'
I put this down to the drink. Yet
once, just once, when there in that
wide cool space, it seemed, backview—

pale mane, legs from waist, skinny jeans—
I saw what you meant but the hawking blonde,
turned front, was a he and clearly offspring
of a greatly different nation.

I found snow still on the lakes patterning
a waiting land. A deliberate people. Three
or four together, they take the air
without hurry, not talking.

Padded against the icy sun, they enjoy
the market square. Old women in their black
buy nothing a lot of the time, just absorb
the windy light, empty-handed.

In a breakfast diversity—rye porridge, Chilean
grapes, more, much more—a hightech Japanese
secured me napkins; 'You're welcome', bowed,
smiled, pat, proud of his universal idiom.

A country for silences, yet an eclectic diet
of languages, empathy with minorities: at the
Archives, we spoke Irish, only, a whole hour
with our young and earnest Finnish helper.

Were you kind to your mother?
And what about the drink?

Saturday Morning

Above, always, the vast dome of clouds
in their perpetual change. I explained
to a visitor from a warm settled clime
such variety was our boon, compensation,
influenced our character. Of course,
I said, it is unwise to generalise but yes,
we are volatile, capricious, astonishing.
However, in my life is a stabiliser:

I have Philip, his procedures unfailing,
he verses me in constancy, tests
at least three times for accuracy.
For thirty-two years I've been apprenticed.

Philip lives on a special plane;
there each question questions
many times in succession.
To answer once does not suffice:
I must equal his stamina.
I am also daring to do things
at my desk; answers tend
to become reflexive and this
stimulates his greater vigour.

Loads of bread? Saturday?
Yes, today is Saturday, loads of bread.
Saturday? *Yes.*
Loads of bread? *Yes.*
Today? *Yes.*
Today Saturday? *Yes.*
Loads shops? *Yes.*

Loads of carrots? *Oh yes.*
Carrots? *Yes.*
Loads cumber: *Yes, loads of cucumber.*
Vegales? *Yes, loads of vegetables.*
Loads of vegales? *Yes.*
Tomorrow Sunday? *Yes, tomorrow is Sunday.*
No shops? *No, only a few.*
No bread? *Yes, some bread.*
No, no bread, no BAKERS.
Oh I see, no, no bakers.
Tomorrow Sunday? *Yes.*

And so it goes, our roundelay.

Suddenly he departs. At my desk
I hear him from the pavement—
passers-by are kind:
No post today? Postal strike?
That's right, Phil, a nuisance.
No post? *No post, Phil.*
He has his appropriate comments:
Jaysus, bloody nuisance!
Indeed it is, Phil …

The voices fade up the slope.
A decent neighbour.
I'll get maybe a half-hour
with my electronic toy.

New Departure

That year you died
I died too. You went
where they put you
into the slant hillside.
I went where acid bent
being into a twisted tomb.

For when you went
I went, knowing only
the end in the end,
the killed years spent
blind corrosively
only hell to tend.

It took five years in all
until the miracle:
having been dead,
I came alive again, saw,
believing newly
hawthorn returned

in flashing miles across
the land, but when the train
took this new departure
you were not. Such a wish,
wish, for—by me—your shape,
delight, as of a child, pure.

Constant Kind

The meeting over, it was late,
their grey heads in the street,
light bones limping from individual causes.

Limp and stoop and unsure direction,
his scant frame, even so, was quick,
linked to his intense talking.

Continually, he turned to her who,
having pointed, looked down, seemed
listening to such insistent exposition.

Crossing to the broken pavement, she
put out a hand, he gave a forearm
which did not cease gesticulation.

Vaguely, they scanned the lane.
As if it mattered not, he parenthesised
for the nearest car of three—

'That's it there: you were right
about that turn'—and at once
resumed his earnest disquisition

on the mysteries of Finnish provenance,
the need of a thorough dictionary when
rendering a language only slightly known.

He spoke on, holding wide the polite door
for her resisting joints, awkward rear,
on, on, while getting in himself.

Walking by her hedge, he was concluding
' … and only in this later time has there
been space for all those early interests.

But the irony, you know …
that push, that urgency for them,
I feel no more.'

He laughed at this,
seemed happy about it.
'Indeed,' she said.

At the street side of her gate
they stood. The merest moment
their faces touched, papery.

Gently they agreed they would
be bound to see each other again
at some gathering or other.

Nothing Heavenly

No Elysian fields, I will just walk out
one day and up that hill that watches Shannon.
At the top I will look back feeling a huge smile.
I will not laugh, need not. I will be liking
it easy, my feet loose of the knots and pits.
At the bottom down there behind me will be
fear, finished, its toxic waste a mystery,
the concern of someone else. I will have
no conscience. I will have done my peculiar
digging, persisted, puzzled at the globe.

Causes of my fear:
      you, the brilliant young who inherit.
             On the hill I will say: You are welcome:
             I too have a heritage—of Nothing.
             I will further say: Nothing, I salute you,
             I love your lack of weight, I have been
             longing for our union.

      you, abstractionists:
             your nothing seemed different,
             showing off, pseudo.

you, materialists who represent
             sleeping in cardboard boxes
             on the streetside of locked doors,
             in alleys, under bridges;
             the reduction of my kin;
             starvation amid plenty.

     our incomprehensible destructiveness

And then having enumerated, I shall remember
my Nothing, shall consider that annihilation
could be various: perhaps on that hilltop
that watches Shannon, the annihilated causes
of my fear and I will easily commingle, smile
our big big smile at the enigma, tell one another
freedom begins only where finishes fear.

Spatial Nosing

Who'll tell the story? you said.
An open issue that but—

Ah love, my love, what are you doing now?
Does the polygamous tendency persist?
I dare say there, wherever it is—
down amid the roots, the laval essences,
out in the measureless voids—it is
a fairly general condition, lightly taken
as breathing. Polyandrous too. That's how
it should have been.

Too bad the way we were conditioned.
How heavily we took all that stuff,
the dark edicts Thou shalt not do this
nor this nor … I'd say it was they
that caused me mealy joints, aluminium hips,
early dentures, fogged eyes since ten.
Bionic woman my grandson calls me.
He is right.

And you, my darling? I suppose your
heaviest afflictions was the pursuit
of cure: it meant panting after it in
all those women, ending up with milky Flo;
the scrutiny of menus whereon were choices
with eclectic names like Whither Appetite?
Vindication of Eros, Reverent Quest,
Why Prostitution? Psyche in Trousers.

I am curious to know how you're doing now
if without pressure of pursuit and search.
Do they blaze a bonfire of inhibitions?
Polygamy for all, polyandry too? Is it very
dull sans tensions? What for incentive?
I'll be nosing spatially one of these days,
under and over and out—five years plus
or so I'd say: you'll fill me in?